Keyboard
Instruments

THE STORY OF THE PIANO

By Lionel and Edith Davis

Illustrated by George Overlie

Prepared under the supervision of Robert W. Surplus

Musical Books for Young People

LERNER PUBLICATIONS COMPANY
MINNEAPOLIS, MINNESOTA

41373

Contents

I Meet the Pianist 5

II Meet the Piano 9

III Look at the Keyboard 11

IV Music on Paper 15

V Play a Tune 19

      RHYTHM 20

      STRESS 21

      ACCOMPANIMENT 21

      VARIATIONS 22

      MUSICAL KEYS 24

      TOUCH AND TONE 28

      SIMPLE BEGINNINGS 29

VI A Harp at the Heart 30

      CLAVICHORD 31

      HARPSICHORD 31

      THE PIANO 32

VII Other Keyboard Instruments 37

VIII You and Music 40

Meet the Pianist

Let's suppose that you have a ticket to the Young People's Concert Series. This is a group of music programs that are specially planned for young people. Next week you will hear a piano recital by a well-known artist. He has planned it for you and others your age.

Let's take a look into his studio this morning. There he is, pacing up and down with a deep frown on his face, instead of sitting at the piano as you would expect, rippling music off the keyboard.

What is the matter? He looks worried. But he shouldn't be. He has been giving recitals for years. He is 35 years old and he has already been studying piano for more than 25 years. Twenty years ago when he was 15, he was practicing for three hours every day, and for many years now he has been spending five or six hours a day at the piano. Certainly you would expect him to play well enough with very little effort.

Still, he is really worried. He is always nervous before a performance. (If you ask him, he will tell you that it is good to be a little nervous. If you don't worry at all, you may not try so hard to do your very best.) But this performance has him more worried than usual.

He feels a special responsibility because you are going to be in the audience. He doesn't know you personally. But suppose one of you has been studying piano for several years and is doing very well. He wants to play the kind of music that will inspire you to work harder and play still better. Suppose another one of you is trying to decide whether or not to begin studying piano. He wants his music to tell you, "Yes." He wants you to get an idea of the many kinds of music the piano can give you.

He has chosen his program carefully:

- A group of 18th century dances by Johann Sebastian Bach written for the harpsichord, before the piano was invented.

- Claude Debussy's magic blending of tones to carry you off into the clouds.

- Frederic Chopin's music played at breathtaking speed.

- George Gershwin's jazz rhythms to set your feet tapping.

When our pianist finishes his program, you will think that the piano can do almost anything.

Now, what about the *encore?* An encore is a piece of music the performer will play for you if you applaud loud and long enough. It is like a little musical gift from him to you. Your applause is your way of telling him that you enjoyed his performance and you wish there were more. The word *encore* is French for "again". "Play again," your applause says. And the pianist sits down, as if to say, "Thank you, there is nothing I enjoy so much as playing for an appreciative audience." And since every artist hopes he will have a really appreciative audience, he will be prepared to play an encore or even two or three.

6

What encore would young people enjoy? Something special. Something very familiar, but something to which the pianist has added a new quality. Our pianist sits down at the piano at last, after all his pacing up and down. He no longer looks worried. He touches the keys, and soon you begin laughing. Because what he is playing could be called "Variations on a Theme," but the theme is —*Chopsticks!* You have heard *Chopsticks* any number of times, and very likely you have played it yourself. But never like this, with interweaving voices and changing harmonies to make the music grow into something much bigger than you ever thought possible.

This is the pianist's gift to you. He is reminding you that the piano is not just for the concert stage. It is your instrument too. He is telling you, "Come on along and join the fun!"

Meet the Piano

The piano is an instrument with many voices. Under the fingers of a fine musician it can seem to do a hundred things. But even under inexperienced fingers it can bring fun and pleasure.

To play a stringed instrument you must train your ear and your fingers to produce the right pitch. To play a wind instrument you must learn to control your breath and tongue to produce a tone. But all the piano asks is that you press down the key, and there you have just the note you were looking for.

It is no wonder, then, that the piano is such a popular instrument. Have you ever tried to count up the different places you have seen a piano? The church basement, the kindergarten, the restaurant, the dance hall, the old barn out on a farm where people come for fun on a Saturday night. And, of course, right in your own living room.

For every piano, there are many pianists. As you would expect, very few become concert artists. But many, many piano students learn to play enough for their own pleasure, to accompany their friends' singing, or to play with the school orchestra. Many find when they get older that they can use the piano in their work. A teacher plays for class songs and games. A music therapist uses the piano in helping sick patients back to health.

There are many pianists who never become concert artists but still have happy careers as full-time or part-time musicians. The ones you are most likely to think of first are your own music teacher, and your church organist. (Almost every organist learned to play the piano before he started to play the organ.) Then there is the pianist you see most often on television—the one who plays as an accompanist to singers and to other instrumentalists, or as a member of an orchestra. The performing pianist may play in *ensembles* (a group of musicians playing together) or he may play alone *(solo)*. The jazz pianist may play with a dance band or with just one or two other instruments in a combo. He may play request music or dinner music.

The pianist may even substitute for an entire orchestra when he plays as a rehearsal pianist. Have you ever thought how much it costs to have an orchestra of 25 or 50 or even 75 musicians play? It is a great saving to pay for only one musician, the pianist, to come to a ballet or musical rehearsal for day-in and day-out practicing. Then, when the dancers and singers are ready to perform, the whole orchestra can be brought in for a few final rehearsals before opening night. No other instrument could do this so well. The pianist can play the parts of the strings, the woodwinds, the brass and even the drums all at the same time. The piano can play higher and lower than any other instrument of the orchestra.

The piano also has other features that make it popular. It is very strong and durable. With proper care it can last for fifty years or more. The slightest blow is dangerous to a precious violin. A wind instrument is easily knocked out of adjustment. But a piano is not nearly so delicate.

A piano wants to be played. If it stands silent, its strings will loosen, its joints will tighten, and its felts may get moth-eaten. If it is played often and tuned whenever needed, the piano will stay in good condition for many, many years. In fact, good pianos are handed down from parents to children and grandchildren in many families.

Look at the Piano Keyboard

When you walk into a room and see a piano, don't your fingers just itch to try it out? Let's!

Take a look at the keyboard. You will see a pattern of groups of two black keys, then three black keys, then two again all along the keyboard. If you start at the bottom of the keyboard (the left end) and play all the white keys one after the other, naming them as you play, ABCDEFG - ABCDEFG, you will notice that each time you play an A or a B or a C it will be in the same position in the keyboard pattern. The white key between the two black keys which stand together will always be D. This pattern is repeated 7½ times on the piano.

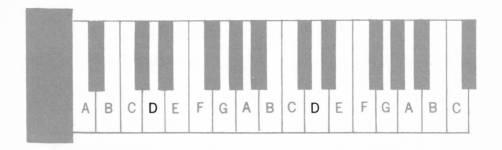

The black keys take their names from the white keys next to them. A black key to the right of the white key is called a *sharp* (♯), and a black key to the left of the white key is called a *flat* (♭).

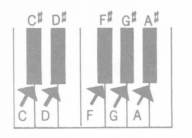

or

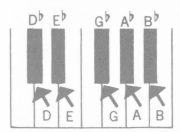

Find a white key named C. The black key to the right of it is called C♯. Now look at the next key, D. The black key to the left of it is called D♭. But it is the same black key, isn't it? So you see that each black key has two names. Now look at the first of the group of three black keys. What would you call it? It is to the right of F, which makes it F♯, and it is to the left of G, which makes its other name G♭.

Interval is the musical term used to describe the distance between keys. In measuring this distance, you count the top and bottom white keys as well as the white keys in between.

12

From C to E is called an interval of a third. From C to G is a fifth. From C to A is an interval of a sixth. Intervals of thirds and sixths are often found in your school song books. From C to C, eight keys, is called an *octave*.

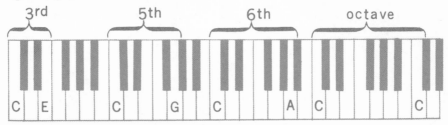

Play the two C's at the same time. Can you hear why these notes have the same name? They seem to be the same sound except that one is higher than the other. You can see, then, that if the sound seems to repeat, the name of the note should also be repeated. This is why the keys are named from A to G and then start at A again.

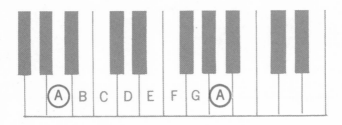

Putting Music on Paper

Many people can pick out a melody by ear. But it would be hard for anyone to play a complicated piece of music unless it were written down. A composer can tell you exactly how he wants you to play his music, not only which notes, but also how loud or soft, and how slow or fast. He tells you all this by musical symbols.

Piano music is written on what is called the grand staff. The grand staff is made up of two staffs, or staves, of five lines each. Each line and each space stands for a different white key on the piano.

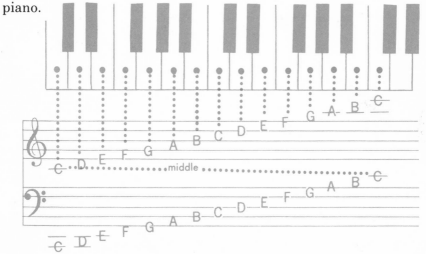

You are most likely already familiar with the upper half of the grand staff, which is called the treble staff. This is marked with the G-clef, and most school children are taught to read music on this staff in second or third grade, because this covers the singing range of their voices. On the piano, the right hand usually plays the music written on this staff.

The lower half of the grand staff is called the bass staff. (This is the range of bass or low men's voices.) It is marked with an F clef. On the piano, the left hand usually plays the music written on this staff.

The grand staff used to be written as many lines, one right under the other.

As you can see, this was very hard to read. So the middle line was taken out. That line stood for middle C. Now, when we want to write middle C we draw a little line between the two staffs to stand for the C line, and on this little line we write the note.

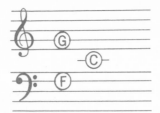

The G-clef sign used to be written as a G circling the G line, the second line up into the treble staff from middle C. The curlicues we are familiar with were added later.

The F-clef sign used to be written as an old style F with the cross line lying on the F of the bass staff — the second line down into the bass staff from middle C.

Do you notice how the curve of the F-clef sign starts on the F line of the bass staff? Another help for you to remember the F line is the two small dots above and below it just to the right of the F clef.

16

If you know how to read and play your bass F, middle C and treble G, you will be able to read and play simple melodies. These notes stand for the F, C and G you find right near the middle of the piano keyboard.

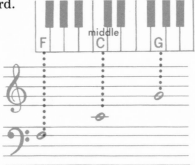

As written notes go up from line to space on the staff, you play up the keyboard to the right, one white key at a time.

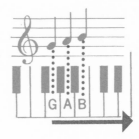

As notes go down from line to space, you play down the keyboard to the left.

As notes skip from one line to the next, you skip one white key and play intervals of a third.

17

Playing A Tune

Now you should be able to take the music from paper to keyboard.

This is how the first line of *Skip to My Lou* is written. You will see a dotted line from the written note to the picture of the key on the piano.

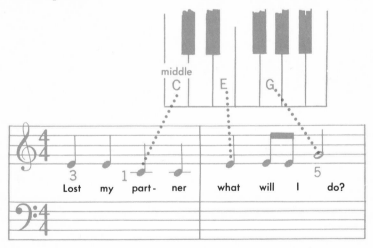

Fingering is planned to make playing more comfortable. If you are playing with your right hand and your melody range is from C to G, it will be natural for you to put your thumb (or first finger) on C, your third finger on E, and your fifth finger on G. This will make the music sound much smoother than if you hopped all around

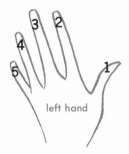
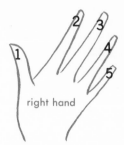

left hand   right hand

the keyboard on one finger, or if you started in a different position and had to twist your hand around to get to the next key. So there are often numbers written right under the notes to help you choose the most comfortable fingering.

Rhythm

The rhythm of *Skip to My Lou* is most likely something you knew without being told. But the written music does tell you the exact rhythm. If you tapped the rhythm something like Morse code you would have this pattern:

Lost   my   part- ner   What will I   do . . . . ?

The different faces on the notes show how long each one should be held. The first notes are quarter notes. ♩ In music written in 4/4 time, there will be four quarter notes in each measure. (A *measure* is the amount of music written between the two long lines or measure bars running down and joining the bass and treble staffs.)

Now for the second measure: The first note for "What" is another quarter note. But "Will" and "I" are quicker. They are two notes played or sung in the time allowed for each one of the quarter notes. Since they are allowed half the time of a quarter note, they are called eighth notes. Eighth notes can be written two ways, either ♪ ♪ or ♫ .

20

The last note, for the word "Do," holds longer than any of the others—twice as long as a quarter note. Two quarters make a half, and this is called a half note. ♩

You could play the whole song more quickly or more slowly, but your rhythm pattern should always be the same. The eighth notes in any song will always be played twice as fast as the quarter notes in that same song, and the half notes will be played twice as slowly.

Stress

If you clap and sing the first line of the song, you will notice that the word "Lost" and the word "What" seem to carry extra strength. This is called *stress,* or *accent,* and it is what makes music dance. The first note of each measure is stressed. The measure bar is a reminder for you that your next note, starting the new measure, should be stressed.

Accompaniment

So far you have played only with your right hand, and the music has been written on the treble staff. Let's add an accompaniment in the bass staff. *Accompaniment* is music that is played along with the melody and "keeps it company."

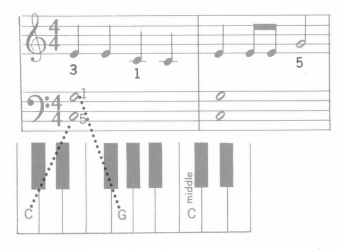

When two or more notes are written one right above the other, they are to be played at the same time. This is called a *chord*. Press C and G below middle C with your left hand at the same time that you press E above middle C with your right hand. Hold these notes. Don't they sound good together? This is called *harmony*. Now play the melody with your right hand while you hold the C-G chord down with your left hand for a full measure. Repeat the same chord for the second measure.

A whole note ○ is a note held for the full measure count of four, exactly as long as four quarter notes or two half notes. Imagine that the lines next to each note in the next diagram stand for the length of time the note is held.

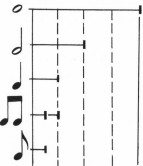

Variations

The whole note chord is a simple accompaniment for our song. We can play our song many different ways, called *variations*. We might play a broken chord accompaniment. This means that each note of the chord is played separately, instead of at the same time.

22

We might play the accompaniment in quarter notes instead of half notes.

Another way would be to play the melody in the bass staff and the accompaniment in the treble staff. With all these changes, or variations, we are still playing *Skip to My Lou.*

You see a new musical symbol in this accompaniment. The curved lines connecting the whole notes to each other are called *ties.* They mean that you hold the right hand chord for the full two measures instead of repeating the chord.

Suppose you would like to play still another variation by moving your melody higher up on the keyboard. You would know what keys to play, of course, because every octave is the same. But how would this be written down on paper?

In order to write music which goes higher or lower than the range of the lines of the grand staff we add little lines called *leger lines* above or below the staff.

You can see that it would be confusing to try to read more than two or three leger lines. If the music is to go still higher (or lower), it is written right on the grand staff with an octave mark over (or under) it to show that it is to be played an octave higher (or an octave lower) than it is written.

leger lines ————————→

is the same as ————————→

Both begin on the third E above middle C.

Musical Keys

There is still another way to vary the song. So far we have been playing it in the key of C, or in the C scale. This means that the melody and chords are based on C as a home tone or foundation tone.

Singing in the key of C might be too low for your voice. Try the key of G. To do this, move your hands up five notes. Your first finger will now be on G. Your song will start on B instead of on E. Does it sound the same?

The first two measures sound fine, but there's something wrong with the F, isn't there? This is because the scale for the key of G uses an F$\sharp$ instead of an F. Look to the next example to see how this is written.

At the beginning of each staff, next to the clef sign, there will be a sharp marked for F. This means that you play the black key to the right of F (F$\sharp$) instead of F all through the song. It is called the key signature.

24

In this accompaniment you see another new symbol. Instead of a note for the fourth beat of the first measure there is a quarter rest. This means that for one beat you don't play anything with your left hand. You *rest* for one beat. A two-beat, or half rest, is written 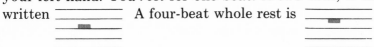 A four-beat whole rest is

Now let's try it in the key of F. Move your first finger to F. The melody will start on A. The F scale uses B♭ instead of B. Remember, a B♭ is the black key just down from (to the left of) B. A flat on the B line in the key signature at the beginning means that you must always play B♭ instead of B.

Each of the examples you have seen has had a slightly different kind of accompaniment. Many, though not all, accompaniments are based on the use of chords. For the last example in the key of F we wrote a little second melody to be played by the left hand at the same time that the right hand plays *Skip to My Lou.* When you play this, you should try the left hand alone a few times to make it easier. It is possible for a pianist to play three, four or even five melodies at one time!

You have heard how certain notes seem to blend well. They can be played together as a *blocked chord,* or the tones can be played one after the other as an *arpeggio* (ahr-PEDGE-ee-o). Arpeggio means like a harp. A harpist will usually play the notes of a chord one after the other instead of plucking all the strings at once.

Put down the right pedal of the piano, and while you hold it down, press the keys for the block chord C-E-G with both hands:

Now, with the pedal down, play the notes one after another. When you are finished with the left hand G, lift your hand and cross it over your right hand to be ready to play the next C as soon as you finish with your right hand G. This is a C major arpeggio. With practice you will be able to play an even flow of music all the way up and down the piano.

(L.H. and R.H. stand for left hand and right hand)

26

Every key has its own scale and its own arpeggio. You have seen the C major arpeggio. The C scale is CDEFGAB and home again to C. The G major scale is GABCDEF♯ G, and the G major arpeggio is G-B-D-G. Try some other scales and see if your ear can tell you when to use sharps or flats. D major uses F♯ and C♯. Did you get them both? Try the D major arpeggio. It uses the first, third and fifth notes of that scale, D, F♯, A and D.

We hear so often about how piano students practice their scales and arpeggios. This is important because scales and arpeggios are building blocks for any piece of music. When you see that a piece of music is written in the key of E major, it might seem hard to try to remember four sharps. But if you have practiced the E major scale and arpeggio, your fingers and your ear will have gotten so used to the sharps that you will play them almost automatically.

We said earlier that fingering is planned to help you play smoothly and comfortably. To get a smooth flow of tones in a scale which has more notes than you have fingers, you will want the most comfortable way of getting your thumb further up the keyboard.

It will be easy and smooth-sounding if you simply tuck your thumb under the palm of your hand after you have lifted it off its first key, and then after you have played the third note with your middle finger, press the fourth key with your thumb again. Now you have enough fingers for the octave.

1 2 3 1 2 3 4 5

Touch and Tone

Have you ever heard anyone say "He has a lovely *touch* at the piano."? This means just what it says. The way your fingers touch the keys will affect the kind of tone you produce. A good touch means a controlled touch, so that you can get just the kind of tone you want.

You must have noticed, as you tried different things out on the piano, that you have produced different kinds of sounds. Some have been loud, some gentle, some smooth, and some choppy. At different times and in different pieces of music you may want to use all these effects. The composer may even tell you how he wants a note played by putting little signs above the note or at the beginning of a song.

Staccato (sta-CAH-toe) notes sound more separated than usual. A staccato mark is a little dot over the note ♪ . When you see this mark you will strike the key sharply and ⎸ pull your finger away as soon as the note has sounded.

Legato (le-GAH-toe) means smooth. A legato phrase will be played so that each key is held down until the next note is about to sound. Your finger will have pressed the second key halfway down before you start lifting the first. A curved mark over a group of notes tells you to play them very smoothly. This is called a *slur*.

The composer will often tell you how loud or soft the music should be. These signs are written between the bass and treble staffs.

p stands for *piano,* or soft, in Italian.
f stands for *forte* (FOR-tay), or loud.

28

You control the tone of your playing by pressing the keys sharply or gently, hard or lightly. Try to see how many different kinds of sound you can get from one note. If you hold your fingers curved over the keyboard and your wrist loose, you will find that your fingers will be springy and you will be able to control your tone very well. If you hold your wrist stiff and your fingers out straight you will be able to do little more than hammer at the keys. This is why a piano teacher spends so much time seeing that good hand position becomes a habit as soon as you start to study the piano.

Simple Beginnings

With the signs we have shown you, the composer can write the most complicated musical instructions. After that it still takes skilled fingers on the keyboard to change the written instructions into beautiful music. But even the most skilled fingers start on their way with a simple song like *Skip to My Lou.*

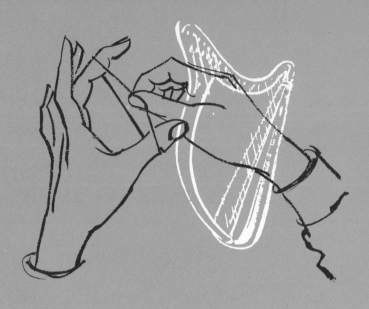

A Harp at the Heart

Have you ever stretched a rubber band and heard it buzz when you plucked it? The buzzing noise is made by the vibration of the rubber band. You can see and feel the rubber band vibrate, and your ears hear the vibration when it is carried to them through the air.

If you stretch and pluck a thin little rubber band you will hear a much higher tone than you will hear from a big, thick one. All stretched strings will vibrate in the same way as your rubber bands. Strings of wire or gut make the best musical tones, and these are the ones that people use for musical instruments.

Short, thin strings give the highest tones, and long, thick strings give the lowest tones. If you stretch a number of strings over a frame, you will have a harp. Hundreds and thousands of years ago, people made music with harps of many different sizes and shapes.

30

Harp strings can be struck or plucked. The zither and the big harp you find in an orchestra are plucked. The dulcimer is a harp whose strings are struck with a pair of hammers, as you would play a xylophone. Keyboards have been used with harps for at least 600 years. You press a key to get a tone from a particular string.

Clavichord

In the clavichord, little brass wedges were struck against the strings when the keys were pressed. It made a very quiet kind of music. The player could play loudly or softly, by striking the keys hard or lightly, but the very loudest was still too soft to be heard very far from the instrument. Because of this, clavichord music was not suitable for public performance.

The clavichord was a small instrument, sometimes as little as two feet long. It could be carried around and placed on a table. It was not expensive, and it was one of the most popular musical instruments for the home in 1500 or 1600. Many old paintings show young ladies seated at the clavichord.

The Harpsichord

The harpsichord was a larger instrument, and since it made louder music it was popular for public performances, either alone or with other instruments.

Instead of wedges to strike the strings, each key was attached to a little pick or quill which plucked the string when the key was pressed.

The quills could be made of different things, such as tiny scraps of leather or feather quills, and cut in different thicknesses. This would make the tone of the plucked string different. A harpsichord could have several sets of quills for each string. The player could change from one set to another by shifting a lever. The harpsichord often had two keyboards, and sometimes it even had two sets of strings, each with several sets of quills. This made it possible to get a number of different tones, brighter and duller, louder and softer. But to change the tone, the player had to stop the music to shift the lever which would bring a new set of quills into position. This meant that he could not play one note loudly and the next note softly, as we can on the piano. He could use loudness and softness only as a contrast between large sections of music. Even when the musician could get contrasts in harpsichord tones, the contrasts were very small, compared to the kind of contrasts we can hear on the piano today.

When we listen to a harpsichord, we notice the unfamiliar, soft, silvery twang of the notes. The instrument is still often used for the music written at the time the harpsichord was popular, when the composers Bach and Handel were living. But it is not at all suitable for keyboard music written after the invention of the piano. In later music, composers paid much more attention to loudness and softness (called *dynamics*).

The Piano

For many years harpsichord makers were trying to solve the problem of how to make it possible for a player to control the kind of sound of each note as he pressed the key. Musicians wanted to be able to express feeling through loudness and softness, swelling and fading music or sudden changes.

At last, in 1709, Bartolomeo Christofori worked out a way to make the tone loud or soft according to the pressure of the finger on the key. This is why our modern piano is called *pianoforte* (soft-loud). From that time on, inventors worked on developing better ways to use Christofori's basic ideas. The modern piano is the result of the work of many different inventors. If you compare a piano with a harpsichord, you will be able to see the long way it has traveled.

You will still find the harp at the heart of the modern piano. It is strung with about 230 steel wires. If you look into a piano you will see these wires. The shortest are very thin and about two inches long. These give the highest tones. The lowest tones come from the longest strings. These are sometimes as much as 80 inches long in a concert grand piano. They have coils of copper wire twisted around them to slow down their vibrations and give them a deep tone.

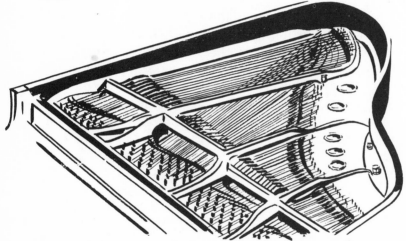

The long, low-pitched wires are louder than the short, high-pitched ones. To balance this difference, the higher notes have two or three wires strung together. This makes them sound as loud, because the hammer strikes them all at once.

One of the important American inventions was the development of the iron frame strong enough to carry the weight of all all these tightly-pulled strings. The pull in a grand piano adds up to between seventeen and thirty tons depending on the size of the piano.

Along the frame you will see rows of tuning pins. The piano tuner uses a wrench to turn these pins and tighten the strings until they give exactly the right pitch. He checks this with a tuning fork and with his well-trained ear.

The harp is mounted on a soundboard. The soundboard is a sheet of wood below or behind the strings. On the soundboard are strips of wood called bridges. Each end of each string rests on a bridge. The vibrations of the strings pass through the bridges and set the soundboard vibrating. This increases the power of the vibrations and makes the music sound louder and deeper.

The *action* of the piano is the arrangement of parts which carry the motion from your finger to the string. Look into a grand piano and you will be able to see how this works. Press down a key. This swings a little felt hammer up to hit a string or a cluster of strings and start them vibrating. At the same time another felt piece is lifted up from above the string. This is the *damper*. The string will continue to vibrate from the blow of the hammer as long as the damper is off. As soon as you release the key, the damper falls back into place and cuts off the vibration. If you press the key hard the hammer will hit the strings hard and make a loud tone. If you press gently the hammer will just tap the strings and make a soft tone. You can also control how long the sound lasts by keeping your finger pressing the key down and holding the damper off the string as long as you like. A quick tap will give a sharp sound, and a long pressure will give a sound that fades away gradually.

On an upright or spinet piano, the same mechanism is turned on its side to work on the vertical strings. There are some changes, because it is working sideways, but the general idea is the same.

Try the pedals and see what happens. The right-hand pedal lifts the dampers off the strings and keeps them off without the keys being pressed. This means that when you press a key and then let it go, the string will continue to vibrate as if you were still holding the key down. If you play a series of notes, they will all be vibrating at once. Sometimes you want to be able to blend your tones, and the composer will tell you when to use this pedal (called *damper*) by the following signs under the grand staff:

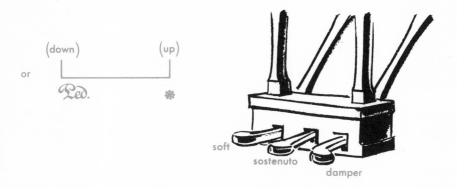

The arpeggios you learned will sound good with the damper pedal down. But if you use the pedal in the wrong places it can turn your music into one big noise, because it will mix tones that do not sound good together.

The left-hand pedal is called the soft pedal (*una corda,* or one string). When you press this pedal, all the hammers shift a little to the right. When you press a key while you hold this pedal down, the hammer will strike only one string instead of the two or three that it ordinarily strikes for each note. With fewer strings vibrating, you will have a softer tone.

The center pedal, called the *sostenuto* (sahs-teh-NOO-toe), or sustaining pedal, holds the damper off some notes but not others. This is helpful when you want to blend your bass harmony but still play a clear melody in the treble. The sostenuto pedal works differently on different pianos, and you have to try each one to see what it can do. Some pianos don't have this pedal at all.

35

These are the pedals that have proven themselves useful in making good music. Many more were invented which are not used today because they did not help make better music. There was once a piano which had a pedal to make drum-like sounds. Another had a pedal for turning pages of the music.

Piano inventors did all sorts of things. One strange piano had a built-in bed and dresser. One folded up for carrying. These inventions are almost forgotten now. But the important inventions are right in our pianos today. There have been no big changes in the last hundred years.

Inventors have not stopped inventing. A popular invention of the early 1900's was the *player piano*. This had a mechanism which could take a roll of paper punched with holes (something like an IBM card), and as the paper rolled along, little pins sliding into the holes would make the proper keys go down. All the player had to do was pump with his feet to make it work, and the keys would go up and down as if invisible fingers were playing them.

A very recent invention is the *electronic piano*. This is a keyboard instrument which has no strings and no soundboard. When you press a key, a hammer strikes a little metal plate which vibrates on pitch, and the sound comes through a loudspeaker. This electronic piano has the advantage of being portable, and it will not go out of tune. But the tone is not very much like a piano.

The insides of standard pianos may not have changed much in the last hundred years, but from the outside they look different now. Modern pianos are made in all sizes. The largest concert grands are nine feet long. The smallest or baby grands are made for the home and they are only five feet long. Upright pianos are now either spinet (less than 39 inches high) or studio pianos which may be about 48 inches high.

Other Keyboard Instruments

The first keyboard instrument was the *pipe organ*. A pipe organ has rows of pipes, a mechanism for blowing air, and a keyboard to send the air to one pipe or another, according to which key is pressed. The first organ in recorded history was made in Greece in 250 B. C. It worked by water pressure, and it had one small row of 20 pipes. Other organs were made in different parts of the world

from that time on. There is a description in an early English manuscript of an organ built in 980 A. D. It had 400 pipes, and seventy men pumped its twenty-six bellows. The monk who wrote about this organ said the sound was so unbearable that everyone put his hands over his ears when it was played.

The organs built in the middle ages and later are very different from this big old noisemaker. In big cathedrals in Germany today you can still hear organs built at the beginning of the 18th century. They are beautiful musical instruments, and modern organ builders still admire their skilled workmanship.

Pipe organs today are built in all sizes. They may have as few as 370 pipes or as many as 40,000 pipes. They may cost anywhere from $5,000 to $150,000. A large organ has many pipes for each key on the keyboard. Each group, or *rank* of pipes, has a different kind of tone, and the organist sets the tone by pulling a knob, or a *stop* for the kind of sound he wants. A very big organ may have as many as seven keyboards, so you can see that by setting each one to play with a different kind of tone, the organist can go from one to the other and get great variety and many combinations in his music. The organ also has a pedalboard which looks like a giant keyboard. The organist plays on it with his feet.

Another kind of organ you can hear today is the *reed organ*. This was very popular in America beginning around 1820. Air was pumped first by foot bellows and later by electric blower pump. The air is blown through reeds instead of through pipes. The reeds are little metal strips attached at one end and free to vibrate at the other end. (A harmonica has this type of reed.)

The *electronic organ* makes its tones with transistors or vacuum tubes. Many different kinds of tones can be set by pressing different levers or buttons. Electronic organs can be very small or very large, though not nearly so large as the biggest pipe organs.

The smallest electronic organ is a *chord organ.* This has a small keyboard to be played with one hand while the other hand presses buttons to play different chords. It sounds something like an accordion.

The *accordion* is pumped with the arms while the fingers of one hand play the melody on a keyboard and the fingers of the other hand press chord buttons. The bellows pumps air through reeds to make the sound. Different kinds of accordions are popular all around the world, especially for folk music.

The *carillon* is a set of bells connected with a keyboard. The oldest carillons had giant keys which had to be pounded with the fists. Modern ones have electrical connections between the keys and the bells.

The *celesta* is made with steel plates which are struck by hammers when the performer plays on the keyboard. A celesta is sometimes used in a symphony orchestra. You can hear it in *The Dance of the Sugar Plum Fairy* in Tschaikovsky's *Nutcracker Suite.*

All these instruments have the same familiar keyboard you have come to know on the piano. Whatever you learn about the piano will help you learn to play other keyboard instruments.

You and Music

Music becomes part of you when you have played even a simple tune by yourself. Playing makes listening more fun, and the more music you hear, the more you want to play. Now that you know a little about how piano music is made, would you like to learn more? We hope you do.

You have seen that the greatest music has simple beginnings, as simple as *Skip to My Lou.* You have seen that anyone can learn to play at least a little.

Many of you will learn to play the piano or some other instrument. Some of you will work hard and long enough to learn to play very well. Your fingers will bring the music of the masters back to life. And perhaps one of you will, in turn, give inspiration to another group of young people just ready to meet the piano.

But in the meantime, all the music in the world is yours. Enjoy it!

ABOUT THE AUTHORS

Lionel Davis has been teaching piano to children for many years. He is also a choir director and organist. His musical career started when he was a boy in Duluth, where he studied piano and played percussion and brass instruments in school bands. He earned a bachelor's degree at the University of Minnesota, and many years later returned for further study in musical composition, voice, organ and piano.

Edith Davis is a writer and editor. She started her career as a "copy boy" at the *New York Herald Tribune* and was later on the editorial staff of *Consumer Reports*. Her articles and stories have been published in newspapers and magazines. She earned a B.A. at Brooklyn College and did graduate work in English literature at the University of Minnesota.

The Davises live in Minneapolis, Minnesota, with their four children. Everyone in the family sings or plays at least one musical instrument, and even the cat likes to curl up on the piano and listen.